Ethical Hacker

VIRGINIA LOH-HAGAN

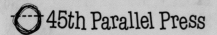

45th Parallel Press

Published in the United States of America by Cherry Lake Publishing
Ann Arbor, Michigan
www.cherrylakepublishing.com

Content Adviser: Ben Miller, ethical hacker, Parameter Security, St. Charles, Missouri
Reading Adviser: Marla Conn, ReadAbility, Inc.
Book Design: Felicia Macheske

Photo Credits: © Subbotina Anna/Shutterstock.com, cover, 1; © Andrey_Popov/Shutterstock.com, 5;
© oliveromg/Shutterstock.com, 6; © Jupiterimages/Thinkstock, 9; © Corepics VOF/Shutterstock.com, 11;
© scyther5/Shutterstock.com, 13; © wavebreakmedia/Shutterstock.co,, 14-15; © Malte Christians/dpa/
picture-alliance/Newscom, 17; © dotshock/Shutterstock.com, 19; © Mark Bowden/iStock, 21; © DIZ
Muenchen GmbH, Sueddeutsche Zeitung Photo/Alamy, 23; © GlebStock/Shutterstock.com; 25, 30;
© Dino Fracchia/Alamy, 27; © pReTeNdEr/iStock, 29; © ARENA Creative/Shutterstock.com, cover and
multiple interior pages; © oculo/Shutterstock.com, multiple interior pages; © Denniro/Shutterstock.com,
multiple interior pages; © PhotoHouse/Shutterstock.com, multiple interior pages; © Miloje/Shutterstock.com,
multiple interior pages

45th Parallel Press is an imprint of Cherry Lake Publishing.

Library of Congress Cataloging-in-Publication Data

Loh-Hagan, Virginia.
  Ethical hacker / Virginia Loh-Hagan.
     pages cm. — (Odd jobs.)
  Includes bibliographical references and index.
  ISBN 978-1-63470-024-5 (hardcover) — ISBN 978-1-63470-078-8 (pdf) — ISBN 978-1-63470-051-1 (pbk.)
— ISBN (invalid) 978-1-63470-105-1 (ebook)
1. Penetration testing (Computer security)—Juvenile literature. 2. Computer networks—Security measures—
Juvenile literature. 3. Computer crimes—Prevention—Juvenile literature. I. Title.

  TK5105.59.L64 2016
  005.8—dc23
                              2015008957

Cherry Lake Publishing would like to acknowledge the work of The Partnership for 21st Century Skills.
Please visit *www.p21.org* for more information.

Printed in the United States of America
Corporate Graphics Inc.

Contents

CHAPTER 1

Helpful Hackers

How do ethical hackers help people and companies? What is a cybercriminal? What is the difference between white hat hackers and black hat hackers?

Shane Kelly set a record. He became the youngest **ethical** hacker. He got trained at age 16. Ethical hackers are computer experts. Ethical means honorable. They're white hat hackers. They hack to help people.

Kelly was bullied. Computers helped him get away.

He took apart computers. He put them back together.

Kelly wants to catch **cybercriminals**. Cybercriminals hack to steal information. Cyber means the Internet. Cybercriminals are black hat hackers.

Computers have **security**. Security protects personal information. Hackers break security. Black hat hackers steal money. They steal information. Ethical hackers test security systems.

Ethical hackers protect people's computers from cybercriminals.

Many houses have security systems. Prisons have security systems. Computers control these systems. Black hat hackers damage these security systems.

One hack opened doors in a prison. Prisoners were set free. This made people scared. Ethical hackers were called. They checked the security.

Ethical hackers help people feel safe in their homes.

WHEN ODD IS TOO ODD!

Some hackers like to prank, or play jokes, on people. Hackers in Montana pranked TV watchers. They hacked a TV emergency alert system. They sent a warning about zombies. The hackers interrupted a TV show. They sent this message: "Civil authorities in your area have reported that the bodies of the dead are rising from their graves and attacking the living. Follow the messages on-screen that will be updated as information becomes available. Do not attempt to approach or apprehend these bodies as they are considered extremely dangerous." People called the police. They were worried. The police told people that zombies weren't attacking. Someone said, "Hacking the emergency alert system is funny until it's not." People need to trust emergency alerts. Pranks like these could harm people.

Tiffany Rad finds security problems. Companies fix these problems. Rad checked prisons. She found many problems.

Rad showed how black hat hackers opened prison doors. She learned how they broke alarms. She found how they changed security videos.

The Lizard Squad is a group. They're black hat hackers. They kicked players out of online games. They said they would shut down gaming over Christmas. They called themselves "the next generation Grinch."

The Finest Squad is another group. They're gamers. They're ethical hackers. They formed to stop the Lizard Squad. The Finest Squad hacked into their social media. They **leaked** their personal information. They leaked the ways they hacked. They put the information online.

Black hat hackers need to be **anonymous**. Anonymous means no one knows who they are. Ethical hackers leak who they are. Ethical hackers want to stop them.

Ethical hackers help people stay safe online.

CHAPTER 2

Thinking Like the Enemy

How do ethical hackers think like black hat hackers? How is ethical hacking legal? How do people become ethical hackers?

Ethical hackers break into computer networks. They break into phones and tablets. They find security problems. They do this before the black hat hackers. They must think like black hat hackers.

Ethical hackers are different from black hat hackers. They test a company's security. They don't misuse personal information. They tell the company what they found.

Black hat hacking is against the law. But ethical hacking is allowed. Companies hire ethical hackers. They give ethical hackers permission.

Companies hire ethical hackers to improve their security systems.

Advice From the Field
JOHN YEO

John Yeo leads a team of ethical hackers. He calls himself a "geek." He loved technology from an early age. Ethical hackers need to be creative. He said, "There is an element of creativity to the mind-set that's required, because it's not just about knowing the technical hows and whys, there is a problem-solving mentality required, you have to think outside the box." Yeo says teamwork is important. He said, "If one person finds an interesting technical problem, the whole team chips in to solve it. It's a good feeling."

Ethical hackers use the same tools as black hat hackers. They use hacking **software**. Software is computer programs.

There's software to crack passwords. There's software to scan for problems. There's software to track how **users** use the Internet. Users are people who go online.

Ethical hackers hack the same way as black hat hackers. They **attack** computers. They get information. They **phish**. They trick people with fake Web sites. They **spoof**. They change e-mails. They fool people. They pretend e-mails come from trusted sources.

Ethical hackers have many tricks. They try to gain access. But they don't steal anything. Black hat hackers steal.

Ethical hackers are always making new hacking software and methods.

A Certified Ethical Hacker has completed a training program.

Ethical hackers get **certified**. Certified means they're official. They get training. They take classes. They take a four-hour test. Some ethical hackers do top-secret government work. They need special permission.

Ethical hackers are technology experts. They understand computer programs. They know how to test, hack, and secure systems.

Ethical hackers follow laws. They are professional. They respect personal information.

Inspired to Hack

Why do people want to be ethical hackers?
What are bug bounties?

At age 5, George Hotz wrote his first computer program. At age 14, he made a robot. At age 17, he hacked a phone. He made it do what it wasn't made to do.

He scrambled the phone's **code**. Code is computer language. He wrote new code. He recorded his hack. He put it on the Internet. Two million people saw his video.

Hotz said, "I hack because I'm bored." He figures out

how machines work. He thinks hacking is a sport. Man against machine. People send him things to hack. He said, "Nothing is unhackable."

Hotz tries to be ethical. He said stealing information is "not cool."

Ethical hackers like to solve problems. They like the fun of hacking.

Spotlight Biography
TSUTOMU SHIMOMURA

Tsutomu Shimomura is a physicist and an ethical hacker. He was born in Japan. He grew up in New Jersey. He's famous for catching a cybercriminal named Kevin Mitnick. Mitnick hacked into Shimomura's computers. Mitnick stole software and e-mails. Shimomura helped the FBI catch Mitnick. He hacked Mitnick's cell phone. He monitored his phone calls. He tracked Mitnick to an apartment. This is where the FBI arrested Mitnick. This real-life adventure was turned into a book and a movie called *Takedown*. Shimomura had a small appearance in the movie. Another book was written about the event. It was called *The Cyberthief and the Samurai*.

Kyle Mallard was a soldier. He fought in Iraq. Now, he fights online. He stops hackers. He defends the United States. Black hat hackers try to steal top-secret information.

Mallard studied computer science. He studied ethical hacking. He continues to serve his country. He said, "I just want to do something where I can look back on my life and say I did good work."

The FBI is a **federal** police force. Federal means it is part of the U.S. government. The FBI hires ethical hackers as cyber special agents.

The government hires ethical hackers to protect our country.

Mike Santillana hacks major companies. He finds security mistakes. He enjoys being an ethical hacker. He said, "We're curious. We want to test our skills. We want to help these companies."

Santillana thinks ethical hacking is like doing puzzles. He likes getting paid for having fun.

Some companies pay **bug bounties**. A bug is a software mistake. Bounties are cash rewards. Companies give money to the first person to find a bug. Sometimes, companies pay thousands of dollars per bug.

Companies learn a lot from ethical hackers.

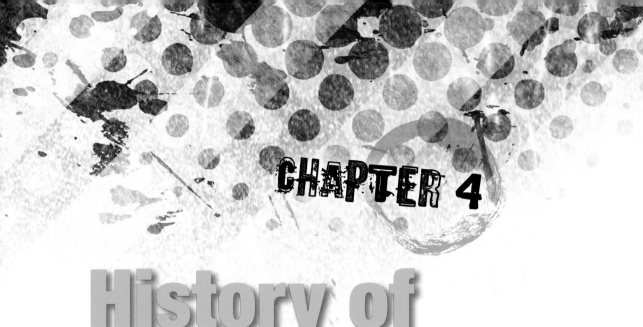

CHAPTER 4

History of Hacking

What are some examples of early hacking?
How did ethical hacking develop from black
hat hacking?

Guglielmo Marconi invented the radio. Nevil Maskelyne
worked on wireless **transmissions**. Transmissions
means the sending of messages.

In 1903, John Fleming used Marconi's invention.
He sent a long-distance message. Maskelyne hacked
into the system. He sent insulting messages. He wanted

to prove Marconi's invention wasn't perfect.

Hackers were useful during World War II. They figured out secret messages.

In the 1960s, computers linked colleges. College students shared what they knew. They made a hacker culture.

Ethical hackers can help win wars.

Ethical Hacker
KNOW THE LINGO!

Botnet: a network of computers controlled by cybercriminals

Brute-force attack: when hackers try to break security by trying all possible passwords, one at a time

Cracking: hacking into a computer without permission

Dictionary attack: when hackers try to break passwords by making a list of words specific to the target and trying those as passwords

Doxxing: publishing personal information to stop people from doing something; public shaming

Firewall: system to prevent unwanted access

Fuzzing: entering lots of random information, or fuzz, in order to crash a system

Malware: bad software

Sniffing: eavesdropping on a network

Spam: unwanted e-mail that tries to get users to buy stuff

Spyware: bad software that collects people's personal information

Virus: a corrupting program that copies itself and spreads from computer to computer

Ethical hacking grew from black hat hacking. Black hat hackers did bad things. Companies needed ethical hackers. Ethical hackers stopped black hat hackers. Some ethical hackers started as black hat hackers.

Kevin Mitnick was a black hat hacker. He's now an ethical hacker. He said, "It is really rewarding to know that I can take my background and skills and knowledge and really help the community."

Mitnick committed cybercrimes. He stole software. He changed networks. He read private e-mails. He was the most wanted cybercriminal in the United States. He was found guilty. He went to prison.

Mitnick's case raised public awareness. People realized the importance of Internet security.

Sometimes, former cybercriminals make the best ethical hackers.

CHAPTER 5

The Fine Line

Who are The Unknowns? How is their behavior both ethical and unethical? What are hacktivists? How are hacktivists both ethical and unethical?

The Unknowns hacked into NASA, the CIA, the White House, and other places. They showed there were problems. They said, "We want to make this whole Internet world more secured because, simply, it's not at all and we want to help." Some believe The Unknowns are a group of ethical hackers.

The Unknowns leaked personal information. Some people thought this was a crime. They thought it was unethical.

The Unknowns admitted to leaking the information. They didn't want to harm anyone. They wanted to force companies to fix their security.

Hackers create cool names. Some of The Unknowns are known as Gricko, The Noob, and Ghostwriter.

Hacktivists hack for political reasons. They hack for social reasons. Some people think hacktivists are ethical. They expose problems of society.

Hacktivists organize online attacks and protests. They support free speech.

Anonymous is a group of hacktivists. They have taken down 40 Web sites that hurt children. But some Anonymous members go too far. They form their own groups. They attack individuals.

What's good? What's bad? There's a fine line between white hat and black hat hacking. Ethical hacking is an odd job.

Hacker wars are when hackers fight against each other.

THAT HAPPENED?!?

Betsy Davies hacked into a computer. She did it when she was 7 years old. She watched an online video about hacking. She hacked it in 10 minutes and 54 seconds. It was part of an experiment. It was part of an Internet safety awareness campaign. Davies proved a point. Public WiFi hotspots can be hacked by young children. WiFi hotspots let users access the Internet. Marcus Dempsey is an ethical hacker. He was in charge of the experiment. He said, "The results of this experiment are worrying but not entirely surprising. ...In an age where children are often more tech-literate than adults, hacking can literally be child's play."

DID YOU KNOW?

- Ethical hackers are also known as "penetration testers." They penetrate, or enter, computers. They test their security systems.

- Cybercrimes are committed all over the world. Every second, there are about 18 cybercrime victims. There are about 1.6 million cybercrimes a day.

- People use the Internet at public places like coffee shops. Hackers can get a lot of information about people in this way. They learn specific information about cell phones. They learn language settings. They learn about the Web sites people visit. They learn people's names. They learn people's passwords.

- Hackers have a hard time hacking strong passwords. Strong passwords have a lot of letters. They use special characters or symbols. They use numbers.

- SWATing has become a popular hacking game. Hackers use social media or computer programs. They trick police departments into sending SWAT teams to people's houses. SWAT teams are special policemen.

- At r00tz, kids learn to become ethical hackers. The Web page says, "Hacking gives you super-human powers. You can travel time and space. It is your responsibility to use these powers for good and only good."

CONSIDER THIS!

TAKE A POSITION! Some people don't like referring to hackers as "ethical." They think hacking is a crime. There aren't any ethical robbers or ethical killers. Do you agree or disagree with referring to white hat hackers as "ethical hackers"? Argue your position with reasons and evidence.

SAY WHAT? There are three different types of hackers: white hat hackers, black hat hackers, and gray hat hackers. Gray hat hackers are not all good or all bad. Learn more about each type. Explain each type of hacker. Explain the similarities and differences.

THINK ABOUT IT! Most ethical hackers work at night. Mikhail Davidov said, "There are few hackers out there who are 'morning people.'" Why do you think this is the case?

SEE A DIFFERENT SIDE! Steve Wozniak is the co-founder of Apple. He understands hackers. He said, "I understand the mind-set of a person who wants to [hack]. And I don't think of people like that as criminals. In fact, I think that misbehavior is very strongly correlated with and responsible for creative thought." Some people think hacking is a crime. Some people think hacking is creative. Which perspective do you agree with and why?

LEARN MORE

PRIMARY SOURCES

The Hackers (BBC Radio Documentary, 2013): www.bbc.co.uk/programmes/p012gp95
We Are Legion: The Story of Hacktivists, a documentary (2012): http://wearelegionthedocumentary.com

SECONDARY SOURCES

Computer. New York: DK Publishing, 2011.
Gifford, Clive. *Technology*. New York: Scholastic, 2013.
Raum, Elizabeth. *The History of the Computer*. Chicago: Heinemann, 2008.
Sande, Warren. *Hello World: Computer Programming for Kids and Other Beginners* Greenwich, CT: Manning Publications, 2009.

WEB SITES

Information Systems Security Association: www.issa.org
International Information System Security Certification Consortium: www.isc2.org

GLOSSARY

anonymous (uh-NAH-nuh-muhs) unidentifiable

attack (uh-TAK) attempt to steal, destroy, or change information off a computer or network

bounties (BOUN-teez) cash rewards

bug (BUHG) software mistake

certified (SUR-tuh-fyed) official

code (KODE) computer language

cybercriminals (sye-bur-KRIM-uh-nuhlz) black hat hackers, hackers who steal information to make money or for bad reasons

ethical (ETH-ih-kuhl) honorable

federal (FED-ur-uhl) relating to the U.S. government

hactivists (HAK-tih-vists) hackers who hack for political or social reasons

leaked (LEEKT) publicly published private information

phish (FISH) attempt to steal credit card information, passwords, or personal details by tricking people into entering personal information on fake Web sites

security (si-KYOOR-ih-tee) protection

software (SAWFT-wair) computer programs

spoof (SPOOF) change the heading of an e-mail or phone number so it looks like it comes from a trusted source

transmissions (tranz-MISH-uhnz) sending of messages

users (YOO-zurz) people who use the Internet

INDEX

ABOUT THE AUTHOR

Dr. Virginia Loh-Hagan is an author, university professor, former classroom teacher, and curriculum designer. Although she loved Keanu Reeves as a hacker in *The Matrix*, she loved him in *Point Break* more. She lives in San Diego with her very tall husband and very naughty dogs. To learn more about her, visit www.virginialoh.com.